THEODORE ROOSEVELT

A Photo-Illustrated Biography
by Steve Potts

Bridgestone Books
an Imprint of Capstone Press

Facts about Theodore Roosevelt

- Theodore Roosevelt was the 26th president of the United States.
- He became president when he was only 42 years old.
- The teddy bear is named after him.
- A likeness of his face is carved at Mount Rushmore in South Dakota.

Bridgestone Books are published by Capstone Press • 818 North Willow Street, Mankato, Minnesota 56001
Copyright © 1996 by Capstone Press • All rights reserved • Printed in the United States of America

Library of Congress Cataloging-in-Publication Data
Potts, Steve, 1956-
    Theodore Roosevelt, a photo-illustrated biography/ by Steve Potts.
    p. cm.--(Read and discover photo-illustrated biographies)
    Includes bibliographical references and index.
    Summary: A brief biography of the twenty-sixth president of the United States.
    ISBN 1-56065-452-X
    1. Roosevelt, Theodore, 1858-1919--Juvenile literature. 2. Presidents--United States--Biography--
    Juvenile literature. [1. Roosevelt, Theodore, 1858-1919. 2. Presidents.] I. Title. II. Series.
E3757.P85 1996
973.91'1'092--dc20
[B]
                                                95-25855
                                                CIP
                                                AC

Photo credits
Archive Photos, cover, 4, 10, 16.
FPG, 6, 8, 12, 18.
Corbis-Bettmann, 14, 20.

Table of Contents

Words in **boldface** type in the text are defined in the Words to Know
section in the back of this book.

Loved by the People

Theodore Roosevelt is remembered as one of America's most active presidents. He had an exciting life. He was a cowboy, a war hero, a police commissioner, a writer, an explorer, a governor, and a president.

He was funny, smart, hardworking, and brave. And he was loved by the American people.

Theodore Roosevelt Jr. was born on October 27, 1858. He came from a wealthy New York City family. His father, Theodore Roosevelt Sr., was active in **civic** affairs. His mother, Martha Bulloch Roosevelt, was a Southern lady.

Theodore was called Teedie as a child. When he grew older, he was called Teddy or TR.

Teddy Roosevelt even has a toy named after him. Teddy was on a hunting trip in 1902 in Mississippi. He refused to shoot an injured bear. Many people thought that was a wonderful thing to do. A toy bear was made and named after him. It was called the teddy bear. Nearly 100 years later, teddy bears are still popular.

Teddy Roosevelt had an exciting life.

Teddy's Family

Teddy was a **frail** child. He was often sick. When he was about 10, his father taught him how to lift weights. Teddy found the weights helped make his body stronger. His mother loved to read to him. Teddy also liked to read and draw animals. He had many pets. Mice, turtles, and birds lived throughout the Roosevelt house.

Teddy liked playing with his brother and sisters. All of his life, Teddy enjoyed writing to his sisters to tell them what he was doing. Teddy's parents liked to travel. When Teddy was young, the family visited Europe and Egypt.

In 1876, Teddy entered Harvard University. He spent many hours studying. He also rowed, boxed, wrestled, and danced.

While he was in college, he met Alice Lee. This beautiful young woman liked Teddy. They married on Teddy's birthday in 1880. A short time later, Teddy started law school. He also won a seat in the New York state legislature. This was the start of a long career in **politics**.

Teddy Roosevelt graduated from Harvard University in 1880.

Out West

Just when life was so good for Teddy, disaster struck. On Valentine's Day, 1884, Teddy's wife died. She had just given birth to a baby girl they had named Alice. On the same day, Teddy's mother died of **typhoid fever**. Teddy was very sad. His friends were not surprised when he went away for a while. Teddy left baby Alice with his sister and went out west to recover.

The year before, Teddy had traveled to North Dakota to hunt buffalo. He loved the west. He rode horses, looked at the landscape, and learned about cattle ranching. He even bought a ranch.

After his wife and mother died, Teddy returned to the west. He needed to spend some time by himself. He created his own **brand** for his cattle. He spent many hours hunting. Some friends traveled with him across the plains. Being away from New York for a while helped Teddy recover. Soon, he returned home. He earned his living by writing books.

Teddy Roosevelt loved the west.

Helping People

Teddy was determined to help people. Between 1889 and 1898, Teddy had three different jobs. His first job was with the Civil Service Commission in Washington, D.C. President Benjamin Harrison appointed him to the job. Commissioners helped the government when it hired people. Many people did not do very well at their government jobs. Teddy wanted to change the way these workers were hired. He wanted to make sure they were trained for their jobs.

In 1895, Teddy returned to New York. There he led the police commission. He made sure the police were honest. Many people in New York City did not trust the police. Teddy changed that. If a police officer was bad at his job, Teddy fired him. People in New York City soon came to trust the police and their police commissioner.

In 1897, President William McKinley chose Teddy for a new job. He appointed Teddy assistant secretary of the navy.

Teddy Roosevelt, center, was police commissioner of New York City.

Sagamore Hill

Teddy liked to spend a lot of time at Sagamore Hill. This was his big house outside of New York City. It was in Oyster Bay, Long Island.

Teddy had married again in 1886. As a wedding gift, Teddy gave his wife Edith the new house. It was named Sagamore Hill after a local Indian chief.

The house had 28 rooms. Teddy had huge bookcases built to hold his many books. Much of Teddy's time was spent writing. Teddy wrote more than 100,000 letters during his lifetime. He also wrote more than 20 books.

Teddy loved to spend time with his children. In addition to Alice, he had five more children. They were Ted, Kermit, Ethel, Archie, and Quentin.

The Roosevelt house was filled with games and sports. People who visited often found Teddy on the floor playing games with his children. The children also had many pets. Once, two of the boys even rode a horse inside the house. They rode it up and down the stairs.

Edith Roosevelt holds Quentin, the youngest Roosevelt child.

The Rough Riders

Teddy became a hero during the Spanish-American War in 1898. Spain ruled Cuba then. Teddy was mad at the way the Spanish were mistreating people in Cuba.

When President McKinley declared war against Spain in April 1898, Teddy quit his job. He became a colonel in the army. He wrote to many friends. He asked them to join him. More than 1,000 volunteers came. Many of these men were Teddy's friends from his days out west. They were cowboys, Indians, miners, and Harvard graduates. They formed Teddy's Rough Riders.

When the volunteers arrived in Cuba, they were ordered to attack San Juan Hill. With Teddy in the lead, the Rough Riders attacked up the hill. The Spanish fired down on them. Dozens of the volunteers were hit by bullets. But the Rough Riders reached the top. The Spanish fled and the Americans took over. Several weeks later, the war ended. The Spanish were defeated. Cuba won its independence. Teddy became a hero.

Teddy Roosevelt's Rough Riders fought in Cuba.

Governor Roosevelt

When he returned from Cuba in 1898, Teddy ran for governor of New York. He won the election.

Teddy found many problems in the state. Thousands of people had moved to New York in the 1880s and 1890s. They came from other parts of the world. There were not enough houses and apartments for all of them. They often ended up living in terrible conditions. Many homes did not have running water, heat, or enough light.

Teddy also found that many businesses did not treat their workers well or pay them a fair salary. Rich businessmen made money by paying workers low wages. Factory conditions were not safe. Women and children who worked there were often mistreated. They worked in horrible conditions.

Teddy was determined to do something to help. He worked to pass laws to make businesses improve. He also helped improve housing and job conditions. He wanted to make sure people would have better lives.

Teddy Roosevelt gave many speeches.

President Roosevelt

In 1900, Teddy was nominated to run for vice president with President McKinley. They won. But Teddy was not vice president for long. In September 1901, McKinley was shot and killed. Teddy became America's youngest president. He was 42.

Teddy ran for president in 1904 and won. He forced businesses to improve conditions. He also attacked illegal **monopolies** called trusts. The trusts had made the price of goods and services too high. The courts backed Teddy.

Teddy loved the outdoors. He set aside large areas as national parks and national forests.

Teddy made the United States a world power. The country built one of the world's largest navies. Teddy backed the building of the Panama Canal. The canal saved ships a trip around the tip of South America.

Teddy also acted as a peacemaker. Russia and Japan had gone to war in 1904. Teddy helped them settle their differences. He won the Nobel Peace Prize in 1906.

Teddy Roosevelt was America's youngest president.

The Last Years

Teddy backed his friend William Howard Taft for president in 1908. Taft won. Teddy planned to retire and spend more time with his family. He also wanted to travel.

Teddy went to Africa. But when he came home he found Taft doing some things he did not like. So in 1912, Teddy ran for president again. He led the Bull Moose party. Teddy lost the election to Woodrow Wilson. But he had presented his ideas to the American people.

When World War I began in 1917, Teddy tried to enlist in the army. He was turned down because he was too old. His sons served, though. Teddy traveled the country to help raise money to fight the war.

By 1918, Teddy was not in good health. He was blind in one eye. His hearing was not very good. And he was very sad. His son Quentin had been killed in the war. After a long illness, Teddy Roosevelt died on January 6, 1919. Many Americans were sad. They missed a man who was one of their greatest presidents.

Teddy and Edith Roosevelt pose with four of their children. Archie and Quentin are in front. Ethel and Ted are in back.

Words from Theodore Roosevelt

"Laws are enacted for the benefit of the whole people, and cannot and must not be construed as permitting discrimination against some of the people. I am president of all the people of the United States, without regard to creed, color, birthplace, occupation or social condition."

From a public statement
September 29, 1903

"The only safe rule is to promise little, and faithfully to keep every promise; to 'speak softly and carry a big stick.'"

From Roosevelt's *Autobiography*, 1913

Important Dates in Theodore Roosevelt's Life

1858—Born on October 27 in New York City

1876—Starts college at Harvard University

1880—Marries first wife Alice Hathaway Lee

1881—Elected to New York state legislature

1884—First child is born; wife and mother die on February 14

1884-1886—Moves to Dakota Territory

1886—Marries Edith Carow

1889-1895—Serves on Civil Service Commission

1895—Named New York City police commissioner

1897—Appointed assistant secretary of the navy

1898—Forms Rough Riders and fights in Cuba

1898—Elected governor of New York

1900—Elected vice president

1901—Becomes president when President William McKinley is killed

1904—Elected president

1906—Wins Nobel Peace Prize

1912—Forms Bull Moose Party; loses election to Woodrow Wilson

1919—Dies at Sagamore Hill

Words to Know

brand—a mark burned onto cattle to signify ownership

civic—of a city or community

frail—physically weak

monopolies—companies that have complete control over the production or selling of products or services

politics—the art or science of governing

typhoid fever—an infectious, often fatal, disease

Read More

Force, Eden. *Theodore Roosevelt*. New York: Franklin Watts, 1987.

Fritz, Jean. *Bully For You, Teddy Roosevelt*. New York: G. P. Putnam's Sons, 1990.

Kent, Zachary. *Theodore Roosevelt*. Chicago: Children's Press, 1988.

Whitelaw, Nancy. *Theodore Roosevelt Takes Charge*. Morton Grove, Ill.: Albert Whitman, 1992.

Useful Addresses and Internet Sites

Theodore Roosevelt National Park
P.O. Box 7
Medora, ND 58645

Theodore Roosevelt Association
P.O. Box 719
Oyster Bay, NY 11771

Theodore Roosevelt
http://csbh.gbn.net/~egy/roosevelt.html
Theodore Roosevelt Home Page
http://www.abcland.com/~jwiedman/tr/index.html

Index